God Jul

AINA STENBERG

BREFKORT.

(ADRESSEN ANBRINGAS Å DENNA SIDA.)

Till Anna-Lisa Cederlund,
Karin Jansson MasOlle och
Torsten Pehrsson med
tack för ovärderlig hjälp.

To Anna-Lisa Cederlund, Karin Jansson MasOlle, and Torsten Pehrsson with thanks for invaluable help.

Skyhorse Publishing books may be purchased in bulk at special discounts for sales promotion, corporate gifts, fund-raising, or educational purposes. Special editions can also be created to specifications. For details, contact the Special Sales Department, Skyhorse Publishing, 307 West 36th Street, 11th Floor, New York, NY 10018 or info@skyhorsepublishing.com.

www.skyhorsepublishing.com

10 9 8 7 6 5 4 3 2 1

Library of Congress Cataloging-in-Publication Data is available on file.

Paperback ISBN: 978-1-5107-6831-4
Hardcover ISBN: 978-1-60239-755-2
eBook ISBN: 978-1-62873-253-5

Printed in China

Previous pages: Aina Stenberg, Eskil Holm, Stockholm 1940 (reprinted 1978).

Cover: Jenny Nyström, Axel Eliassons Konstförlag, Stockholm 1908.

Design: Anders Neumuller
First published by Bonnier Fakta 1978

The reproduction rights for the Jenny Nyström and Curt Nyström Stoopendaal-motifs in the book were obtained from Axel Eliasson AB Konstförlag, and the Aina Stenberg motifs from Karin Jansson and Britta Yngström.

Anders Neumuller

God Jul

A Swedish Christmas

Skyhorse Publishing

Max Hänel, Granbergs Konstindustri AB, Stockholm.

Contents

Ellen Björklund, Centraltyckeriet, Stockholm 1907.
The card was an insert in the Midwinter Christmas
magazine that was published by Frölén & Comp., Stockholm.

When You Are Waiting for Something Good...

The Celebration of the Year   It is no coincidence that in Sweden the most important celebration of the year takes place during the darkest and most inhospitable season of the year. Christmas brightens Swedish life and gives us something to look forward to during the rest of the year. Christmas traditions have changed almost entirely during the last four to five generations. Many of what are considered to be ancient traditions, handed down from generation to generation, were actually unknown to Swedish forefathers. We have let go of customs that have lost their significance and acquired new and imported ones that we feel have added something more meaningful to the celebration of the year.

The Visual Christmas Ideal   One of Sweden's youngest traditions is the Christmas card. It would be hard to imagine Christmas without them. When Swedes conjure up a picture of Christmas in their imagination, they see something that has been depicted on a Christmas card. The background and the people may be a bit different, but the set-up has been available for sale on a 4 × 6-inch piece of cardboard. Swedish image of a real Swedish Christmas has been shaped by decades of holiday cards. This is where the Christmas goat, the Christmas buffet, the Christmas pig, Santa, the Christmas tree, the early morning church service—yes, even the Christmas spirit first appeared in a picture format and gradually became Swedish visual ideal of Christmas. The Christmas celebration is a romantic quest for more secure times of the past. This nostalgic quest is also one of the reasons why we see so few entirely modern Christmas cards. Publishers try to introduce more international motifs and contemporary artists, but most people still choose older, beloved motifs from Christmases past.

Facing page:

TR-n (Torvald Rasmussen),
Le Moine & Malmeström
Konstförlag, Göteborg 1904.

J.C. Horsley, R.A., Joseph
Cundall of New Bond Street,
London 1846 (1881).

Anonymous German card with
glitter, 1892.

AF (Alfred Schmidt), 1895.

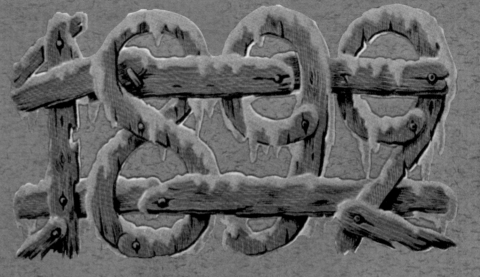

The First Christmas Card How did the Christmas card come about? There are many theories. Greeting cards in some form or another have actually been used throughout the ages. At the time of the birth of Christ, the Romans sent palm leaves or small gifts to each other as a symbol of victory and success. In Japan there is a very old tradition of giving Surimono cards to friends and relatives on the Japanese new year. (The explorer Sven Hedin had a Chinese New Year's greeting card from 300 A.D. in his collection.) The oldest European new year's greeting still in existence dates back to the 14th century. Toward the end of the 18th century names day cards became popular in Germany. Each calendar day was dedicated to a saint and, on the day, you would send greeting cards to any acquaintances who had the same name as the saint. This was much easier than trying to remember birthdays. Half a century later, the first new year's card appeared in England and it was not many years after this that Henry Cole ordered the very first Christmas card in 1843. Sir Henry—his title derived not from the invention of the Christmas card, but for his founding of the Victoria and Albert Museum—had started a phenomenon. The artist John Calcott Horsley depicted the yuletide message with a happy family seated around an extravagant Christmas meal. Three generations—children, parents, and grandchildren—raise their glasses in a toast to a merry Christmas and a happy New Year. The temperance lobby of the time protested against the motif and were not appeased by the vine-framed side panels showing the less fortunate being fed and clothed. The card was printed in 1,000 copies that were individually hand-colored by the artist. Just two Christmases later, the Royal Mail distributed 25,000 Christmas cards.

GODT NYTT ÅR!

IDUNS REDAKTION

En glad Jul!

The Golden Age of the Christmas Card   Starting off as a rather exclusive phenomenon, the Christmas card got its big breakthrough in the 1760–70s when people in large parts of Europe started sending them to each other. One reason for the spread of this custom was that the price of the cards and the postage came down considerably. At the same time, introduction of oil printing meant that the chrome lithographic method replaced hand-coloring. The foremost artists of the time were engaged and competitions with large cash awards were announced to bring in new motifs. In England alone, as many as a quarter of a million different motifs were produced as Christmas cards before the turn of the century.

Tulle and Silk Ribbons   The very first Christmas cards were sent or given to the recipients in envelopes just like normal letters. The envelope made it possible for the card to be decorated with pressed flowers, tulle, velvet cut-outs, cloth appliqués, silk fringes, and reliefs in gold. Snow and ice was depicted with glitter made of glass or metal, cotton wool, and tin foil. The card would sometimes incorporate a mechanism that changed the picture, or three-dimensional components that could be folded out. Realistic imitations of cigarette butts, false teeth, bacon, corkscrews, hairpins, and coins were popular. What connection these had to Christmas was anybody's guess.

Anders Olsson, Sagokonst,
Stockholm 1948.

Adele Söderberg, Axel Eliassons
Konstförlag, Stockholm after 1910.

Swedish Christmas Cards When the postcard was introduced toward the end of the 19th century, the postal service had to bring in extra staff to handle the flood of Christmas cards. Competition between publishers increased and the artistic quality declined. The least expensive production was in Germany, and subsequently large parts of Europe were consuming German angels, Santas, and rather monotonous winter landscapes. It took a long time for Swedish Christmas card publishers to free themselves from the German dominance. The Danes were somewhat more successful, and for this reason there are many old Swedish Christmas cards that read *Glaedelig Jul* instead of *God Jul*. The essentially Swedish Christmas cards only started appearing after the turn of the last century. They became so successful that Swedish motifs were sold in Scandinavia, Russia, Estonia, Latvia, Lithuania, and in the Swedish settlements of North America.

GOD JUL!

·SIGNE·ASPELIN·

God Jul.
Önskar af Mamma
o. Pappa.

Signe Aspelin, Axel Eliassons
Konstförlag, Stockholm after 1910.

German Christmas card imported
by Åhlén & Holms Konstförlag,
Insjön 1905.

Christmas, a Harvest Festival   The winter season is taxing. In the countryside, the progressively shorter days had to be filled with more and more work. The climatic conditions in the Nordic countries meant that a good harvest could never be taken for granted, and therefore there was no celebration until the threshing was done. And that was around Christmas time. For Swedish forefathers, this was the end of a long and hard year of work, without any vacation. At last, all the stores were filled and it was time to enjoy the fruit of their labor. This was the Christmas of the agrarian society and of past times. In Sweden there have never been special harvest celebrations of the kind they have in southern Europe in the fall, so a Swedish Christmas is essentially an old harvest festival.

The Timing   "And it came to pass in those days, that there went out a decree from Caesar Augustus that all the world should be taxed." These are the first lines of the story of Christmas (Luke 2:1). But the events that are retold did not actually take place at the time of year that we celebrate it today. Celebrating the birth of Christ in December has a pagan background. We do not know exactly when Jesus Christ was born, but historically the day has been defined as January 6. When Christianity was introduced in the Nordic countries, the newly selected time for Christ's birth coincided with the pagan Midwinter sacrificial feast. From the Midwinter feast, we have only retained the copious eating and drinking and the word *Jul*. Jul has probably also existed in other Germanic languages but has been Christianized to Christmas (Christian mass) and *Weihnacht* (the holy night).

Anders Olsson,
Bacco 1965.

Jenny Nyström, Axel
Eliassons Konstförlag,
Stockholm 1905.

The Waiting Game   The time leading up to Christmas has always felt extra long for children. Countless are the wish lists that were written during this time. To help them count the number of days left until Christmas, children are given advent calendars. The first such calendar was published in 1934 by the League of Swedish Female Scouts and designed by the famous Christmas card artist Aina Stenberg MasOlle who continued to do the design for the next thirty years. Eventually, Walt Disney and Swedish television started producing other popular versions of the calendar. Ten years before the advent calendar, the advent candlestick was introduced to enable adults to count the days left until Christmas.

AINA STENBERG

GOD JUL OCH GOTT NYTT ÅR!

God Jul!

Må julen fröjd och lycka ge,
Och må du många ljus i Jul få se,
önskar. - - - - -

329

Busy Times

Christmas Preparations   The first preparations for Christmas used to start during the summer. That is when the curdling of the Christmas cheese was done, and toward the late summer, nuts were collected for all the sweets. Apart from this, most of the main tasks were saved until November. Animals were to be slaughtered, *lutfisk* prepared, and Christmas beer brewed. At the same time the farmer had to get in and thrash the harvest, dig up the potatoes, and pick the last of the vegetables. The fields had to be prepared for the spring sowing and all the tools checked and stored away. Then there was all the firewood that would be needed for the long winter ahead—just one of the myriad tasks that needed to be completed. You have to wonder what we have to complain about these days.

Useful Gifts   Swedish forefathers seemingly had an informal open-house format for their celebrations. The more formalized generosity probably came with the Christian influence. Households always had to have gifts in preparation for visitors as no one was to leave the house empty-handed. During a time when the economy was based on subsistence production, bread was the most common gift, but food items, aquavit, fabric, and candles were good substitutes. Tenement soldiers, pastors, parish clerks and any employees were also paid in kind, while the parish poor were given a taste of the bread.

Jenny Nyström

God Jul!

1032.

274

En bunt ljus på julafton från din vän

Previous page:

Aina Stenberg, Eskil Holm, Stockholm 1946.
Anonymous 1905–1910.

Jenny Nyström, Axel Eliassons Konstförlag, Stockholm 1909.

Anonymous, Le Moine & Malmeström Konstförlag, Göteborg 1910.

Lit Candles   Lit candles have become one of the most important ingredients of the Christmas celebration. This came about only after electric light became commonplace. Prior to this, candles were an everyday necessity, and candle-making was part of the normal Christmas preparations. Candles with branches were used to spread light on the Christmas table. Candles with three branches were christened "Trinity Candles." Originally, each family member was designated one branch of the candle and how long and bright each branch burnt became one more way to foretell the future. Above all, the burning of the branches predicted whether it would be the master of the household or the mistress who would die first.

After the electric light had lost its novelty value, it was largely precluded from the Christmas celebration. Churches that used electrical lighting (even with electronic flickering) during the rest of the year, turned it off during the Christmas holidays. Today with a greater awareness of the hazards of fire, electric lights are the norm on Christmas trees as well as on window decorations.

En glad Jul!

Christmas Baking   About a week before Christmas, it was time to start baking. First in line were the gingerbread cookies as they did not need to be fresh. Called *pepparkakor* (pepper cookies) in Sweden, they used to be baked with real pepper and not specifically for Christmas. Saffron buns, which today are a Christmas specialty, were also eaten year-round. Special for Christmas at that time were the shapes given to the saffron buns and the gingerbread cookies which were also used as Christmas tree ornaments and decorations. Apart from shapes like roosters, pigs, horses, hearts, stars, men, and women, the gingerbread dough was also used to make entire landscapes, with houses, churches, and carriages that were kept until the Christmas tree was stripped and thrown out at the end of the holidays with a party. The pig, by illustrator Einar Nerman, and the other decorative animals were originally symbols of fertility, appearing as growth demons.

B.E. (Britta Elfström)

Lisa Lindbergs,
Granbergs
1891–1905.

L.B., Eskil Holm,
Stockholm.

Aina Stenberg,
Eskil Holm, Stockholm.

E.K-K., Paul Heckscher
1920.

Einar Nerman,
Nordisk Konst.

God Jul! *Nllonskat din kollega...*
Eneret. A. V. Kbhvn. *ser au grisen slår hull på...*

Eneret, A.V. Köpenhamn
1891–1905.

Anonymous 1905–1910.

Slaughter On Anna's Day, December 9, it was time to soak the lutfisk. This was also the first time the Christmas beer could be tasted. The slaughter had already begun, especially for sheep and cattle which would only get progressively thinner as the winter season set in with a vengeance. For the pigs, the situation was the opposite: It was better to slaughter them as close to Christmas as possible to allow them to get fatter. The cheerful, fat pigs on many a New Year's card were somewhat of an anomaly but also indicative of the pig having become a Christmas symbol with a value beyond the Christmas table.

Piggy The main figure of Christmas is definitely Santa, but the pig is a strong runner-up. The Christmas goat ranks third, at best, in the Christmas hierarchy among mythological figures, all of which were outdistanced by children, especially on Christmas and New Year's cards. The pig is often depicted as Santa's friend and close associate. The more human-looking the pig, the closer is his relationship with Santa and humans. Indeed, in the olden days the gingerbread man and gingerbread woman were called Nisse and Nasse, respectively. Nisse is the Swedish word for the legendary good-natured elf, while Nasse is the nickname for a pig. On one of her cards, Jenny Nyström even painted a *Nisse & Nasse AB* on a truck indicating a pig helping Santa transport Christmas gifts. That pig had definitely risen through the ranks! Today, Nasse has merged with Nisse into Santa's helper.

GLAD JUL!

Jenny Nyström, Axel Eliassons Konstförlag, Stockholm 1906.

Anonymous embossed Danish card from 1911.

Christmas Card Motifs   "Flowers, Santas, everything possible and impossible from the whole world, from all seasons have been forced to become part of the Christmas card," laments Gleeson White in his book, *Christmas Cards and Their Chief Designers* (1895). He plowed through some huge Christmas card collections. The largest British collection encompassed 163,000 Christmas cards in 700 albums weighing over 6 tons.

As time went by, Christmas card producers had a better idea of what sold, and the huge variety in motifs diminished. Since almost all Christmas cards undergo aesthetic consideration before they are sent, they are a very good reflection of people and the culture they live in. Hence, the Christmas pig's evolution from the ham to family happiness has a significant symbolism.

Christmas Card Psychology   In Great Britain, the Christmas card phenomenon was given serious consideration, and British psychoanalysts even claimed to be able to read the character of a person by his or her choice of cards. The results published in 1963 are not that sensational: "Large Christmas cards are sent by people who have an inferiority complex or are afflicted with some type of exhibitionism."

Jenny Nyström,
Axel Eliassons
Konstförlag,
Stockholm 1911.

Anonymous
German card.

Jenny Nyström,
Axel Eliassons
Konstförlag,
Stockholm 1902.

Jenny Nyström, Axel
Eliassons Konstförlag,
Stockholm 1902.

Anonymous, C.N:s
LLj., Stockholm 1946.

Jenny Nyström, Axel
Eliassons Konstförlag,
Stockholm 1908.

Glad Jul!

God Jul
tillönskas af YOU

Jenny Nyström,
Axel Eliassons
Konstförlag,
Stockholm 1907.

Jenny Nyström,
Axel Eliassons
Konstförlag,
Stockholm 1904.

"Christmas cards on glossy stock indicate that the sender is a happy, pleasant, and very peaceful person who lacks the ability to concentrate." Hence, Christmas cards with velvet applications, to give special emphasis to the pattern, are selected by people who are particular about making an impression but could, according to experts, also be an indication of mistrust, jealousy, purposefulness, and obstinacy. Patterns where the color blue dominates are chosen for the most part by intellectuals with strong imagination. Darker colors are chosen by those with a sensitive nature. Red patterns are popular among women, the reason being that red is a strong force of attraction. Men who choose red Christmas cards are regarded as henpecked husbands or, at best, as dependent on others and longing for a motherly, dominant woman. Yellow Christmas cards indicate that the sender is an egotist or a recluse, with a longing for tenderness. Orange is selected by sociable individuals, and lilac by pompous people. "'Funny' Christmas cards are generally sent by people who are not very funny themselves." Now what does a card with a Christmas pig say about the sender?

Christmas Greetings When the first Christmas cards made an appearance, three quarters of the population lived in the countryside. The cards grew in popularity in step with a large-scale migration from the countryside to the cities. Or to America. However painful this process was, it was important to give it a positive spin, especially to those left behind, and the best way to do this was with a postcard. Cards were convenient because they only left room for a short message. It was cheap; the card cost five öre and the postage four öre. These factors together created a veritable postcard craze all year-round but especially at Christmas and New Year. Initially, Christmas and New Year's cards were delivered on the actual days. Cards that were mailed well in advance were sorted and kept in special boxes. There are many stories of invitation cards being mistakenly sorted as Christmas cards to the annoyance of hosts and hostesses.

Telegraphy and Telephony Eventually, the need for speed gave birth to telegraphy to be followed later by telephony. There were not many Christmas and New Year's greetings exchanged by telegram, but the Christmas card artists were quick to introduce these modernities in their motifs. Children listening to the faint sound of the telephone lines, illustrates a belief in the future that was universal at this time. There may not initially have been many telephone lines leading into the cottages, but you can be sure that the telephone had become a must-have for the next generation.

Aina Stenberg, Eskil Holm, Stockholm. The card served as an envelope for a message inside.

Aina Stenberg, Eskil Holm, Stockholm 1924.

Jenny Nyström, Axel Eliassons Konstförlag, Stockholm 1910.

Lisa Lindberg Fröman, Granbergs 1903.

Max Hänel, Ernst G. Svanström Dt. 1904.

Lisa Lindberg Fröman, Granbergs 1903.

Jenny Nyström,
Axel Eliassons
Konstförlag,
Stockholm 1908.

Jenny Nyström,
Axel Eliassons
Konstförlag,
Stockholm.

God jul!

God Jul! önskar Axel.

The Christmas Tree   The Christmas tree became commonplace in Sweden through its depiction on Christmas cards by Jenny Nyström and other artists. In really old Christmas cards the "continental" Santa, St. Nicholas, arrives with gifts for the nice children and twigs for the naughty. As a reminder of this, children were often given a twig in a jug of water that would blossom as Christmas neared. Later on, it became customary to decorate the twig with apples, gingerbread cookies, and candles. The step from twigs to Christmas trees was not a big one. The Christmas tree, like many other Christmas customs, was a German import.

Anonymous.

Anonymous, P.F.B. 1906. The card was addressed to a passenger onboard the steamship Prins Gustaf.

Anonymous German card from 1905–10.

Jenny Nyström, Axel Eliassons Konstförlag, Stockholm.

A. Sjöberg, Tullbergs Konstindustri AB 1896.

Jenny Nyström, Axel Eliassons Konstförlag, Stockholm 1909.

I den snöiga nord
Finns ett land på vår jord,
Som vi hålla så innerligt kärt.
Där bor kraft uti arm,
Där blir hinden så varm,
Där har ungdomen mandom sig lärt.

GOD JUL!

Anonymous German card printed in Saxony.

Outdoors In the olden days, the snow always lay invitingly white and unspoiled right up to the doorstep. Christmas was a time for outdoor fun that included tobogganing, skating, skiing, and sledding. Adults and children alike made snowmen, snow lanterns, and fortresses, and threw snowballs at each other. Santa was not spared.

Jenny Nyström,
John Fröbergs
Förlag.

27

"Snowball card"
by Jenny Nyström,
Eskil Holm,
Stockholm.

"Miniature card" by
Aina Stenberg, Eskil
Holm, Stockholm.

"Tip-top-card" by
Aina Stenberg, Eskil
Holm, Stockholm.

Opposite page:

Jenny Berg 1916.

J.N.
(Jenny Nyström)
without the
publisher's name,
circa 1902.

28

God Jul!

Jenny Berg

Godt Slut

Godbörjan

tillönskas af

Winter Amusements

Snowball Cards Irregularly shaped Christmas cards have always been popular. The snowball inspired Jenny Nyström to create a collection of "snowball cards" in the early 1900s. The inventive Aina Stenberg, who designed the depicted "tip-top-card" and "miniature card," also made a few cards with mechanisms. These were all echoes of the 19th-century penchant for imitations and fantastic materials and punched-out shapes. The motif was secondary and often more of an ornament added to accentuate the material. These cards were expensive to make and required an envelope, and they disappeared when the simple and standardized postcards became the norm. In later years, the expensive, dressed-up cards made a comeback as folded cards have overtaken postcards in popularity. The fold was originally introduced to make it easier to showcase Christmas cards on mantelpieces in British and American homes.

The World's Largest Christmas Card Among the most unusual Christmas cards ever sent was the one received by the Prince of Wales in 1929. A small grain of rice contained not only the address but also a greeting and a picture of a car. The world's largest Christmas card was mailed in 1968. It was six miles long, weighed two tons, and was a greeting from soldiers who had returned from the Vietnam War to their comrades still serving in the war. It was delivered in the form of a paper roll by a specially chartered plane.

Jenny Nyström,
Axel Eliassons
Konstförlag,
Stockholm 1906.

Jenny Nyström,
Axel Eliassons
Konstförlag,
Stockholm 1906.

Card Series A Christmas card artist has to design four to ten different cards each spring for that year's production. The photographers that the card producers employed had to produce as many possible motifs in a single day. They really had to make full use of the scanty ideas, models, and settings they had at hand. It is therefore not unusual to see the same man drink to the New Year first with a blonde, then with a brunette, and so on. Series of two to ten cards with a short story were also produced. The "erotic cards" at the turn of the century were also sold as collectors' series. The cards with motifs of an advancing flirtation, exploited with a great deal of sensitivity the erotic charge in tobogganing, swinging, or other couple situations outside the bedroom.

Glædelig Jul.

Glædelig Jul.

Glædelig Jul.

Glæd

Gott
Nytt År

Two anonymous series
of German cards.

Hildur Söderberg,
Granbergs.

Hildur Söderberg,
Granbergs.

Proessdorf,
accompanying
the *Julhälsning*
magazine from
Nordiska Förlaget
in Stockholm 1913.

Jenny Nyström,
Eskil Holm,
Stockholm 1905.

Anna Palm de Rosa,
Eskil Holm 1905.

A.H., Granbergs
1925.

32

Anonymous 1903.

Jenny Nyström,
Fröbergs 1902–1904.

Dorothea Johansson

God Jul
tillönskas af
Kersti Persson

Child Motifs   Christmas is above all a holiday for children. It is also through children that Christmas becomes more meaningful for adults. Jenny Nyström loved to paint children. In her portrayal of her son Curt and his friends, there is an expression of innocence, goodness, and happiness. There are no naughty or troublesome children on Christmas cards. And that is why we can't help loving them. They live in the elucidated shimmer we want to remember Swedish own childhood in.

Mature Beauties   The children that are portrayed outdoors are more natural than those in the rather stuffy, interior scenes. It is also outdoors that we encounter young adults—who seem to be proscribed inside. The three young beauties are unique and could probably only have been depicted outdoors and in connection with a sport.

Anna Palm de Rosa   The young skier in the "landstorm" uniform, with the Swedish flag in the background, was popular in 1905. The card was painted by Anna Palm, the artist most closely connected with the early Swedish postcards. Her watercolors, with different city motifs, are among the most sought-after by Swedish and foreign postcard collectors. Anna Palm, born in 1859, was the daughter of a landscape painter. She added "de Rosa" to her name after her marriage to an Italian officer.

Aina Stenberg-MasOlle,
Eskil Holm, Stockholm.

Jenny Nyström, Axel
Eliassons Konstförlag,
Stockholm 1910.

Leading up to Christmas

Lucia Several Nobel laureates have been frightened when they have been woken by the beautiful song of the candle-bearing Lucia in their room at Stockholm's Grand Hotel on the morning of December 13. The coffee and the saffron bun have been good compensations for the rude awakening. Lucia is the only uniquely Swedish Christmas tradition. The first Lucia was likely an angel with wings and a crown with lighted candles as a halo in an end-ofterm Christmas play. In earlier figures of Lucia, the wings are still on but the candles are on a tray. Adopted as a tradition by the upper class, Lucia spread to universities and schools before it evolved into a public Christmas celebration that is a must at every place of work and school all over Sweden on December 13. The tradition became official when *Stockholms-Tidningen* in 1927 turned it into more of a pageant. The export of Lucia has also been very successful.

Lucifer   Lucia has been adorned by the legend of Santa Lucia as well as the Lucia song which, in the original Italian version, is all about the port of Naples. In medieval times, the night of Lucia was the longest of the year and therefore favored by the devil and his followers. Lucia, and its much older predecessor, Lusse, have, in all likelihood, as strong a connection with Lucifer—the devil, as with Lux—light, in Latin. The shape of the saffron Lucia bun (*lussekatt*) probably stems from a cat being one of the many shapes that the devil could take on when he visited mortals.

Anonymous 1912.

Kerstin Ornö, the Stockholm Lucia in 1952. She was chosen in a competition in *Stockholms Tidningen* and photographed by Bergne.

God Juls Tillönskos

Jenny Nyström

Anonymous 1903.

Jenny Nyström,
Axel Eliassons
Konstförlag,
Stockholm
19th century.

Tomas Day   December 21, Tomas Day, was a traditional market day. In the past it was a day the "Christmas peace" set in. Anybody who continued to work after this day could be befallen by the most terrible mishaps. The only ones who were allowed to work were the pastor and all supernatural beings. On Tomas Day, everybody dressed up in their Sunday best for a visit to the closest market. But before leaving the house, there had to be a traditional sip of the Christmas beer which by now had fermented to perfection. One of the items that was to be purchased at the market was aquavit, that is if it had not already been brewed at home. The market visit was by tradition a "wet" affair and the day was popularly called "Tomas Drunkard" (Tomas Fylletunna).

Christmas Market   At the Stortorget market in Stockholm, there were 95 vendors in 1838. Apart from the trinkets and fancy goods booths, there were bakers, sheet metal workers, bookbinders, brushmakers, jewelers, hatters, toy sellers and soap makers,

Gott nytt år!

ANNE CH: SJÖBERG.

God Jul
önskar Mathilda

God Jul!

God Jul

GOTT NYTT ÅR

God Jul!

Anne Ch: Sjöberg.

Anonymous with German text on the back, 1903.

Anonymous.

Helge Artelius, Axel Eliassons Konstförlag.

Jenny Nyström, Axel Eliassons Konstförlag, Stockholm 1907.

37

Jenny Nyström,
Axel Eliassons
Konstförlag,
Stockholm 1908.
The card has a
greeting in Finnish.

Anonymous,
Ferdinand Hey'l,
Stockholm 1900s.

Jenny Nyström
1906 (no publisher's
name).

Jenny Nyström,
Axel Eliassons
Konstförlag,
Stockholm 1905.

V. Schonberg,
Svenska Litografiska
Anstalten.

Jenny Nyström,
Axel Eliassons
Konstförlag,
Stockholm.

Curt Nyström
Stoopendaal,
Axel Eliassons
Konstförlag,
Stockholm 1907.

Jenny Nyström,
Axel Eliassons
Konstförlag,
Stockholm 1925.

instrument makers, basket weavers, and many more. The market gave the farmer an opportunity to make some money from the products of the farm and spend it on all kinds of Christmas specialties. The grocer had fruits and other delicacies that were impossible to get during the rest of the year. There was a great choice of Christmas tree ornaments and decorations for the home. There were Christmas stars made of paper or straw to hang at windows, and textile hangings to decorate walls and ceilings. Many Christmas card artists also produced an annual paper version of the hanging. Plaster of Paris churches that could be illuminated were highly treasured. There was, of course, no lack of all kinds of carnies, carousing and general merrymaking at the markets. Children were treated to cotton candy or hot dogs from Helge Artelius' impressive booth.

The Commercial Christmas   These cards are a reflection of the modest beginnings of the commercial Christmas. The Christmas markets really only sold such goods that could not be made at home. The upper middle class attire of those carrying the parcels tells us that the purchase of such goods was the reserved privilege of but a few. The purchases were normally carried home by porters, so the parcels on the cards are more a symbol of the merry abundance of Christmas than a real life situation.

Goe Jeel!

JULKLAPP!

God Jul!

Elsa Beskow,
Axel Eliassons
Konstförlag,
Stockholm 1913.

The signature THS,
Åhlén & Holm.

Elsa Beskow In the book *Petter och Lottas Jul* by Elsa Beskow, we read about how Lotta crocheted and sewed all her Christmas gifts while Petter made his from wood. Afterward, they packaged their gifts in lots of paper and sealed them, so that there would be lots of suspense when the parcels were opened. Lotta looks a lot like the little girl with the stick of sealing wax on the Christmas card above.

Elsa Beskow was an artist, painter, and author who created the classic Swedish illustrated children's book. When she, around the turn of the century, became the art teacher at the Whitlock School in Stockholm, she started illustrating Christmas magazines. Later, between 1912 and 1914, she also created lots of beautiful Christmas cards.

Aina Stenberg,
Eskil Holm,
Stockholm 1939.

H Söderberg,
Svenska
Litografiska AB,
Stockholm.

Sealing Christmas Gifts   The smell of the bright red sealing wax is, for many Swedes, the ultimate smell of Christmas. But these days, most Christmas gifts are packed by store assistants when they are bought, and the intricate packing, the wax sparkling in the candle, the spitting on the seal and the satisfaction of achieving a perfect seal are becoming a thing of the past. And not many Christmas rhymes are written any longer either.

An Evening of Preparations   In the past a family, sometimes joined by farm employees and their families, would gather together for a "stay-up-evening." This was on a normal work night and did not really have anything special to do with Christmas. The radio program "Only Mother is Awake," hosted by Maud Reuterswärd, popularized the idea of a "stay-up-evening" before Christmas when the family gathered around the kitchen table to pack Christmas gifts, make ornaments, and prepare toffee and other goodies.

G. Stoopendaal,
Calegi Sto.

Isaac Grünewald,
Axel Eliassons
Konstförlag,
Stockholm.

Jenny Nyström,
Axel Eliassons
Konstförlag,
Stockholm.

M. Hänel 1901.

Jenny Nyström,
Axel Eliassons
Konstförlag,
Stockholm 1925.

Anders Olsson,
AB Ingvar Larsson.

The Christmas Sheaf   Christmas is a time when generosity toward both people and animals abounds. In the old days, every visitor was to be treated to food and drink, otherwise they would rob the home of Christmas. The sheaf, put out for the birds as another symbol of this benevolence, is a motif on numerous Christmas cards including one by the famous painter Isaac Grünewald. The sheaf is a remnant from heathen times when the spirit of the harvest was believed to remain in the last sheaf harvested. This sheaf was raised on a high stake in the yard to bless the family, the animals, the earth, and all worldly possessions.

Opposite page:

ID 1907.

Colored
photograph,
K.V.i.B.,
Köpenhamn 1903.

Anonymous 1902.

Anonymous,
Axel Eliassons
Konstförlag,
Stockholm 1909.

Anonymous photo,
RP.

G. Stoopendaal,
Nilssons
Ljustrycksanstalt,
Stockholm 1915.

G. Stoopendaal,
Nilssons
Ljustrycksanstalt,
Stockholm 1910.

Colored photograph
from Axel Eliassons
Konstförlag,
Stockholm.

44

Come All Ye Santas

St. Nicholas Older Santas look a lot like Greek priests. They are tall and grand with imposing beards. St. Nicholas was a bishop in Asia Minor in the year 300, who, after his death, became one of the most popular saints, especially with schools, children, and travelers. When his day was celebrated in Catholic schools on December 6, the good students got praise and presents from St. Nicholas while the bad students got a symbolic taste of the rod by the little devil figure that accompanied him. Eventually the two figures merged, but the question "Are there any good children here?" that all Swedish kids are asked by Santa, still serves as a reminder. Nicholas was so popular that he survived the reformation to become Sinterklaas in Holland and Santa Claus in the English-speaking world.

The Swedish Santa The *jultomte* in Sweden is a mixture of St. Nicholas, other foreign Santa figures, and the *tomte* of Swedish folklore. He was a house spirit of Germanic origin, who brought the farm and its inhabitants luck, even if he had to steal it from the neighbors. Viktor Rydberg defined the tomte's character in the story *Little Vigg's Adventure on Christmas Eve*, in 1871, and ten years later in the poem *Tomten*. Jenny Nyström, who illustrated both the story and the poem, started combining Nicholas, the German Christmas man, Snow White's seven dwarfs, Kilian Zoll's first Swedish Santa in 1851, and all the other little gnomes to create the Swedish Santa.

Jenny Nyström,
Axel Eliassons
Konstförlag,
Stockholm 1912.

Jenny Nyström,
(no publisher's
name).

Jenny Nyström,
Axel Eliassons
Konstförlag,
Stockholm.

Jenny Nyström,
Axel Eliassons
Konstförlag,
Stockholm.

Curt Nyström
Stoopendaal,
Axel Eliassons
Konstförlag,
Stockholm.

Anders Olsson,
AB Ingvar Larson
Konstförlag.

Jenny Nyström,
Axel Eliassons
Konstförlag,
Stockholm 1902.

Jenny Nyström
(no publisher's name)

Jenny Nyström When the 17-year-old Jenny Nyström read *Little Vigg's Adventure on Christmas Eve* in *Handelstidningen* in 1871, she got so inspired that she proceeded to illustrate it. When the story was published as a book, it was Nyström's Santa drawings that were used even though the author Viktor Rydberg did not think that they matched his picture of Santa. When Jenny Nyström later illustrated the poem *Tomten*, she used her father as a model and a different type of Santa emerged. It was quite similar to Nyström's teacher Fredrik Wohlfart's Santas, but eventually got a profile of its own. All kinds of Santas of all ages emerged that were up to all kinds of things like cycling, driving cars. jumping with parachutes, or listening to the radio.

Jenny Nyström (1854–1946) had started a promising traditional artistic career as a portraitist and landscape painter. She studied at Konstakademien in Stockholm, in Munich and in Paris and, already in her youth, received the much-coveted Royal medal. But her serious painting at the easel has been completely overshadowed by her enormous production of illustrations and cards. For these, she has done literally thousands of clever variations of a limited number of Christmas motifs and motifs with children, a true testimony of her creativity. Many artists, including her son Curt Nyström Stoopendaal, followed her lead. The cards and small posters of the mother and son are sometimes hard to tell apart.

Aina Stenberg,
Eskil Holm,
Stockholm 1939
(72, 74, 76).

Aina Stenberg,
Eskil Holm,
Stockholm 1939
(64, 72, 73, 74, 76).

Aina Stenberg,
Eskil Holm,
Stockholm 1939
(64, 72, 73, 74, 76).

Aina Stenberg,
Eskil Holm,
Stockholm 1948.

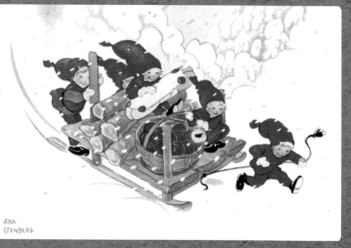

Aina Stenberg,
Eskil Holm,
Stockholm 1951
(78).

Aina Stenberg,
Eskil Holm,
Stockholm 1947
(75, 78).

God Jul och Gott Nytt År!

God Jul och Gott Nytt År!

Aina Stenberg MasOlle   Jenny Nyström was undoubtedly the leading Christmas card artist with a naturalistic style, but when it comes to the decorative school, the foremost representative was unarguably Aina Stenberg. She varied two motifs to perfection on cards, runners, napkins, placement cards, posters, and advent calendars. Her signature small Santas and the beautiful "national cards," with colorful provincial costumes, were inspired by the summers and Christmases spent in the folkloristic province of Dalarna where Aina Stenberg's husband, painter Helmer MasOlle, grew up. Aina Stenberg painted a couple of thousand motifs, selling her first Christmas motif for one krona at the age of 18 and ending her painting career in her 90s when she was beginning to lose her eyesight. While Aina Stenberg's lead pencils were sharpened until they were like needles, her watercolors were soft and fresh. The effect of this was further enhanced as her cards were hand-lithographed in eight colors. Her motifs got simpler and cleaner as she aged.

Aina Stenberg,
Eskil Holm,
Stockholm 1936.

Aina Stenberg,
Eskil Holm,
Stockholm 1936.

GOD JUL OCH GOTT NYTT ÅR

G. Stoopendaahl,
Carl Nilssons
Ljustrycksanstalt,
Stockholm.

Aina Stenberg,
Eskil Holm,
Stockholm 1957
(1978).

Anonymous 1905.

Anonymous 1906.

Haddon Sundblom   Curiously, the artist who gave the world its picture of Santa Claus, was not represented on a single Christmas card in Sweden. Haddon Sundblom, with Swedish-Finnish roots from the island of Åland, became a very successful commercial artist in Chicago. His first Santa Claus appeared in an advertisement in the *Saturday Evening Post* in 1931, and for the next 35 years he created new Santa ads each year for the Coca-Cola Company. Just as Jenny Nyström used her father as a model, Sundblom, who painted in the same classical style as Anders Zorn, based his Santa on a retired salesman who had the right build and "the wrinkles in his face all seemed to be happy wrinkles." When the salesman passed away, Haddon Sundblom used himself as a model because by then his broad, Nordic face also had the same kind of happy wrinkles. A Swedish kid's image of a Santa today may very well resemble the one Haddon Sundblom created for Coca-Cola, rather than a traditional tomte. But then there is a true Nordic connection hidden away in those wrinkles.

Little Santa   In North America and Great Britain, children get their gifts on the morning of Christmas Day. In Germany, children wake to find all their unwrapped gifts under the Christmas tree. In Sweden, many children get a few small gifts, from Little Santa, in their stockings on the morning of Christmas Eve. This keeps them busy until the real Santa arrives after dinner. Yes, to this day, almost all Swedish children get a visit from a flesh-and-blood Santa on Christmas Eve—a uniquely Swedish tradition. In days of old, many children also got a gift in advance on Tomas Day, which was celebrated as "Little Christmas" with a pre-taste of all the food and drink that was waiting to be consumed on Christmas Eve.

Anonymous 1883.

God Jul

AINA STENBERG

Christmas At Last

Decorating the Christmas Tree Before the Christmas tree became common in Sweden, around the turn of the last century, it was customary, in the countryside, to decorate a tall candle holder. Made out of wood, it was covered in red and green paper before apples and candles were added. When the spruces took over, they were decorated quite differently by the various social stratifications. A farm laborer's Christmas tree could, as its only decoration, have cotton wool meant to look like snow on the branches. A tree in a wealthy home in the city, meanwhile, would be covered with paper-wrapped candies, marzipan figurines, cookies, apples, birds of glass, flags, candles and hearts of plaited paper holding nuts, or other goodies. Figurines in the form of dogs, cats, bells, children, and flower baskets were often hung from a loop of thread. Made out of sugar and chalk by the local baker, the figurines were hard as stone and hardly edible, to the disappointment of all children. The confectioner's marzipan figurines, on the other hand, often made their way straight to the candy buffet. The tree had to be topped with a flag or a star. The popularity of the flags posed a real problem for Christmas card producers. It was, for instance, impossible to sell pictures of trees decorated with Swedish flags to the Danes. The artists solved this dilemma by either drawing all the Nordic flags on the tree or, at times, by changing the flags for each individual country. The spirit of internationalism on Christmas cards today is quite obviously a surrender to commercial considerations, with a single motif serving as many markets as possible.

God Jul!
Godt nytt år!

GOD JUL.

God Jul!

God jul!

God jul!

Previous page:

A.M. Eneret.

Aina Stenberg,
Eskil Holm,
Stockholm 1948.

Ellen Björklund,
accompanying
the Christmas
magazine *Midvinter* in
1906, published by
Fröléen & Co in
Stockholm.

Lisa Lindberg
Fröman, Granbergs
1891–1905.

T R-n
(Torvald Rasmussen),
Le Moine &
Malmeström
Konstförlag, Göteborg
1905.

Jenny Nyström
in a series
of *Förgätmigej* cards.

Jenny Nyström,
Axel Eliassons
Konstförlag,
Stockholm 1907.

Jenny Nyström,
Axel Eliassons
Konstförlag,
Stockholm 1909.

The Final Preparations   When the Christmas tree was decorated and little Christmas posters covered as many of the walls and ceilings as possible, the floors were covered with straw. In urban areas, the preferred covering was spruce branches, but eventually the insurance companies pulled the brakes on this custom. Not only did the house have to be spic and span, people also had to be squeaky clean for Christmas. For many, this involved the first and last full bath of the year. On farms, everybody took a bath in order according to their family ranking, in the same water. After the bath, new clothes, or clothes that had been part of the big Christmas wash, were put on. When this monumental task was completed, it had to be topped off with several shots of aquavit. Bring on Christmas!

All Decorated and Ready   Christmas cards never depict all the nitty-gritty work involved in the Christmas preparations. Everything is always magically decorated and perfect. We see the master of the house light the last candle on the perfectly dressed tree while children and adults look on starry-eyed. If it ever looks like a lot of work, there is always a little Santa ready to step in and help. And if the Santas are otherwise occupied, there are helpful angels, on older cards, ready to lend a hand. The guardian angels were let loose by a papal decree in 1883 so that they could fly and help out in all kinds of situations.

Anders Olsson,
Sagokonst 1946.

Jenny Nyström,
Axel Eliassons
Konstförlag,
Stockholm 1912.

E. Torsslow,
Svenska
Litografiska AB,
Stockholm
after 1910.

Anonymous
pre-1905.

Anonymous
German card 1912.

Anonymous, EAS
1907.

Jenny Nyström,
Axel Eliassons
Konstförlag,
Stockholm 1905.

Jenny Nyström,
Axel Eliassons
Konstförlag,
Stockholm 1906.

Jenny Nyström,
without any name
of publisher.

Anders Olsson,
Ingvar Larsson
Konst AB.

Jenny Nyström,
Axel Eliassons
Konstförlag,
Stockholm 1913.

Anonymous,
Axel Eliassons
Konstförlag,
Stockholm.

Offering by Nonbelievers Something that comes with every Christmas celebration are the complaints about how expensive and stressful it all is. This raises the question of how a small farm in the countryside had the resources to replace its austere and strenuous daily life with one of abundance and idleness, albeit, for only a few days. Anthropologists liken the excesses of food and drink at Christmas with Pagan offerings. The offering was the prayer of primitive peoples. By having lots to eat and drink, and by being excessively benevolent toward visitors and the poor, nonbelievers hoped that the same abundance and benevolence would be afforded to them by the powers above.

The Ringing in of Christmas At last, the peace of Christmas could be heralded by church bells or a christened tomte. This was the signal to cease any fights or petty quarrels for the duration of the holiday season. This prohibition was even stated in Sweden's ancient provincial laws. Crimes of violence during the Christmas holidays were more severely punished than those committed at other times of the year.

Anders Olsson The artist who continued to paint Christmas cards in the traditional way for the longest time was Anders Olsson, with his characteristic decorative signature. He was as careful with details as Jenny Nyström, and this gives his numerous cards and small posters, with settings from the 1950s and 1960s, added value. Check out the fireplace! Anders Olsson's anatomical skills, so evident in his nude studies and his illustrations of "Red Indians," have been put to good use on his more muscular Santas.

God Jul

TOMTEN.

Glömsk af sele och pisk och töm
Pålle i stallet har ock en dröm:
krubban, han lutar öfver,
fylls af doftande klöfver.

N:o 4. Serien omfattar 10 motiv ur "Tomten" af Viktor Rydberg.

JENNY NYSTRÖM

ENERET J.F.

T R-n
(Torvald Rasmusson),
Wilh. Lundkvist,
Stockholm 1909.
The card was number 4
of 10 with text from the
poem *Tomten* by Viktor
Rydberg.

Jenny Nyström,
Eneret 1899.

Santa's Reward   The tomte of Swedish folklore worked hard everyday. He had the well-being of the farm in his hands, and he would take this supernatural power with him if he moved so he had to be treated well and with a lot of sensitivity. Apart from this, all he demanded in return for his goodwill, was an annual bowl of porridge. Originally, this was put out for the tomte on New Year's Eve, but after his status was raised to that of Santa, the annual reward was given on Christmas Eve. It was not only Santa who got a treat on this day; all the animals were given extra rations. The guard dogs were taken off their leashes and were even allowed to taste the Christmas porridge.

Jenny Nyström,
Axel Eliassons
Konstförlag,
Stockholm.

Jenny Nyström,
Fröbergs, Finspong.

G. Stoopendaal,
Svenska Litografiska
AB, Stockholm.

Jenny Nyström,
Axel Eliassons
Konstförlag,
Stockholm 1909.

Aina Stenberg, Eskil
Holm, Stockholm
1945.

Jenny Nyström,
Axel Eliassons
Konstförlag,
Stockholm.

När gröten kokas av en liten gumma,
Den smakar ljuvligt som kardemumma.

God Jul

Hedvig Rosendahl

AINA STENBERG

It's Christmas Time

The Christmas Pile   On Christmas tables of old, a pile of baked goods was laid out at each setting as a form of a placement card. Sometimes names were written in sugar on the top of a wheat bun. The master of the house got the biggest Christmas pile while the rest were in proportion to each person's ranking in the household. The servants were given extra big piles as they shared them with their families. There were many symbolic values attached to the bread which was baked and shaped in accordance with ancient recipes. On top of the master's heap, there was often a loaf in the shape of a small bird with an ear of wheat in its beak and a wish for a good harvest in the coming year. The bread from the pile was not to be eaten right away and some of the baked goods were to be saved until after Christmas.

The Christmas Menu   It is simpler to list what was not on the Christmas buffet, than the other way around. The conspicuous absentee was potatoes, as they were consumed every other day of the year. The Christmas menu was dominated by the products from the newly slaughtered pig. Nothing was wasted, and the dipping of bread in the gravy, fresh ham, ribs, pigs' ears, and all the other delicacies must have been a wonderful break from a daily diet of salted and dried meat or fish. Fresh fish was not readily available at Christmas, but pickled herring and lutfisk were on the menu. During the Catholic era, only "white" food was eaten during the days leading up to the big holidays. Both the lutfisk and the Christmas porridge are remnants from that time. Porridge was eaten year-round, but rice porridge was reserved for festivities.

Previous page:

Hedvig Rosendahl.

Aina Stenberg,
Eskil Holm,
Stockholm 1947.

Jenny Nyström,
Axel Eliassons
Konstförlag,
Stockholm 1908.

Jenny Nyström,
Axel Eliassons
Konstförlag,
Stockholm 1906.

P. Lindroth,
accompanying
the *Julhälsning*
magazine from
Nordiska Förlaget
1913.

Adéle Söderberg,
Axel Eliassons
Konstförlag,
Stockholm.

Anonymous,
Svenska Litografiska
AB, Stockholm
1912.

Jenny Nyström,
Axel Eliassons
Konstförlag,
Stockholm.

Carl Larsson,
Förgätmigej kort
1973.

M.L. Borgh,
Axel Eliassons
Konstförlag,
Stockholm 1900–06.

H. Larsen,
Paul Heckschers
Förlag.

Jenny Nyström,
Axel Eliassons
Konstförlag,
Stockholm 1908.

Adina Sand,
Granbergs 1917.

Jac. Edgren,
Nordisk Konst.

62

Aina Stenberg,
Eskil Holm 1947.

Angel Food The night of Christmas Eve was one of the most magical of the year. This was when an almond in the porridge could reveal who was going to get married. But before tasting the porridge, each person around the table had to recite a "porridge rhyme." All the food was left on the table because there was a belief that the recently deceased would come down for a taste on this special night. Eventually, this custom was Christianized and a little extra food was laid out as "angel food." It was not unusual for a place to be set at the table for family members who had died during the year.

Aina Stenberg,
Eskil Holm,
Stockholm.

Jenny Nyström,
Axel Eliassons
Konstförlag,
Stockholm 1910.

Jenny Nyström,
Axel Eliassons
Konstförlag,
Stockholm 1909.

Colored
photograph,
Åhlén & Holm,
1915.

German card from
1921.

Jenny Nyström,
Nordisk Konst 1965.

Fellowship and Devotion   Family and servants gathered for prayer and the singing of hymns before the more secular and merrier aspects of Christmas began in earnest. The master of the house read the gospel, and the real meaning of Christmas was proclaimed. Older Christmas cards very often have a religious theme, and about a quarter of cards today still come with a religious message. Apart from scenes of the family gathered around the bible and motifs inspired by the Last Supper, there are cards with Jesus in the crib, the expedition to the Christmas Day morning church service, landscapes with churches, a ringing church bell, and angels. When a family gathering is depicted on a card, it most often comes with all the upper middle class trimmings. Just as in contemporary family photographs, the handsome parents and well-behaved children are captured in stiff poses.

Anonymous,
Alex. Vincent's
Kunstforlåg,
Eneberettiget.

C. Hedelin's
"Skånsk jul,"
Tullbergs
Konsindustri AB
1895.

Photo by Gerda
Söderlund,
Axel Eliassons
Konstförlåg,
Stockholm 1910.

Gold-embossed
card, PBF, 1911.

Hildur Söderberg,
1917.

Colored
photograph.

M. Dellhagen,
Knut Bobecks
Vykortsförlag,
Stockholm before
1906.

Anonymous card
with printed sender,
1891–1905.

Anonymous,
1905–1910.

Colored
photograph.

Colored photograph
from Austria.

Jenny Nyström,
Axel Eliassons
Konstförlag,
Stockholm 1900.

Hannes Petersen,
HWB, 1930.

Jenny Nyström,
Axel Eliassons
Konstförlag,
Stockholm 1912.

Jenny Nyström,
Axel Eliassons
Konstförlag,
Stockholm 1916.

Jenny Nyström,
Axel Eliassons
Konstförlag,
Stockholm 1906.

Jenny Nyström,
Axel Eliassons
Konstförlag,
Stockholm.

Jenny Nyström,
Axel Eliassons
Konstförlag,
Stockholm 1906.

Jenny Nyström,
Axel Eliassons
Konstförlag,
Stockholm 1904
(reproduction of
older motif).

Jenny Nyström,
Axel Eliassons
Konstförlag,
Stockholm 1915.

Santa Arrives   At last he is here, the long-awaited Santa. And in Sweden, he comes to the house in person. He does not look much like he does in the pictures, but he is here. It has been a full year of toil for all the small "nissar" or gnomes who make the toys and other gifts in the Christmas gift factory at the North Pole or in Lappland. The same toys are strangely enough available in the stores downtown. Mum and Dad have apparently bought the gifts in the store but Santa helps to distribute them. And he comes from far away to do that. As usual, Dad misses Santa's visit as he is away on a last-minute errand. And Santa is always in a hurry as he has to make it to so many children's homes. He is warmly thanked as he waves goodbye and leaves with his empty sack. Eventually Dad returns and is so disappointed that he once again missed Santa's visit.

Anonymous, EAS
1910.

Hand-painted card
from the Stockholm
Postal Museum
collection, 1917.

Jenny Nyström,
Axel Eliassons
Konstförlag,
Stockholm 1917.

Anonymous, EAS.

Jenny Nyström,
portrait of son Curt,
1906–1908.

Jenny Nyström,
Axel Eliassons
Konstförlag,
Stockholm.

E. Blomberg,
Jolin & Wilkenson
Konstförlag, Göteborg 1918.

Anonymous, Axel Eliassons
Konstförlag, Stockholm 1903.

The Christmas Gift   Gift giving at Christmas has a very modest beginning. It may all have started with the St. Nicholas gift on December 6. Or it could have been the New Year's gift that was so popular at one time but has now completely disappeared. Or it might have started with the tasty treats that servants and others received at Christmas. But the origin could just as well have been the little humorous rhyme or funny object that was given anonymously with a bit of gamesmanship. The idea was to knock on someone's door on Christmas Eve or on one of the following days, quickly throw in the so-called gift on the floor, and make a quick getaway. The recipients, pursuing the giver, more often than not in vain, would in turn try and get rid of the embarrassing gift in the same way so as not to be the final butt of the joke. In Swedish, the Christmas gift is called *julklapp* which literally translates into the "Christmas pat" on the door.

The Christmas Goat   One of the most popular dress-up clothes for men in the olden days was to wear the fur coat inside out, that is with the fur lining on the outside. With horns and a beard added and a special gait to boot, you had a perfect goat. This is how the little devil, who accompanied St. Nicholas on his gift-giving expeditions, was dressed. Before Santa came around toward the end of the 19th century, the goat had taken on the important role of the distributor of gifts in Sweden. Today the goat, made of straw, has been relegated to a popular Christmas decoration in all Swedish homes. There have historically been attempts to have Little Jesus or the angels bring the gifts but Santa seems to have emerged as the undisputed victor in this competition.

T R-n
(Torvald
Rasmussen),
Eskilstuna
Fotografiska
Magasin, Eskilstuna
1904.

Anonymous, 1912.

Anonymous, SB,
1914.

Anonymous
German card, 1909.

Robert Högfeldt,
1957.

Anonymous likely
British card, 1905.

T.H. Tesch, 1917.

Toys The earliest toys given as Christmas
gifts were wooden figures and dolls made out
of straw. They were very primitive compared
to the toys that were beginning to be produced
in factories. The pretty playthings on the
Christmas cards were the domain of privileged
children. For others these were the subject of
dreams that they could closely study on the
cards they received. There were dolls with
the most precious little porcelain faces and
exquisite wardrobes. After 1870, there were
also ingenious mechanical toys produced in
Germany. Tin soldiers and swords were some
of the many popular military toys. But this was
also a time when just a pen and paper would
have been very gratefully received.

Robert Högfeldt Then as now, toys were
chosen by the parents. So a father dressed up in
a Santa suit playing with the mechanical train,
while the children look on, is probably quite a
true-to-life image. Dutch-born Robert Högfeldt
was skilled at coming up with hilarious settings
for his small and plump jovial figures. His
lithographic posters are now being rediscovered
just like a lot of other popular art that did not fit
into the criteria of serious art of the past.

73

Opposite page:

The signature H.B., A.V., Copenhagen 1904.

Amalia Lindgrens "Dance in the Dalecarlian cottage," H.L.J., Stockholm 1902.

Semmy Nyström, Granbergs 1915.

Anonymous, AB Oscar E. Kulls Grafiska Konst-Anstalt, Malmö.

G. Stoopendaal, Sv. Litografiska AB, 1914.

Jenny Nyström, Axel Eliassons Konstförlag, Stockholm 1908.

The signature T.N., G.K.A. 1904.

G. Stoopendaal, Åhlén & Holm, 1900.

The Fox Scuttles Over the Ice

Dancing Around the Christmas Tree

Dancing around the Christmas tree is obviously a tradition dating back not longer than the Christmas tree itself. However, even before there was a tree, there was always dancing and games after the sumptuous Christmas meal. Servants socialized with their masters on an equal footing during the democratic Christmas holiday. The wooden clogs stayed on even indoors as the carpets had been replaced by straw. It was fun to romp around on this comfortable flooring. Men excelled at different games of strength while the whole family joined in for games like *Blind Man's Buff* and the Swedish dance games Skära, Skära Havre and The Fox Scuttles over the Ice, which are mentioned as early as the 17th and 18th centuries. Most homes had very little space, so most of the serious dancing took place at the communal parties or "playhouses" as they were also called. This is where youth, old enough to have been confirmed, met to dance, play, and consume all the food and drink that they had collected after a little begging from the adults.

Georg Stoopendaal
The happy couple dancing in the kitchen, as well as the Santas' ring dance were produced by Georg Stoopendaal. His Christmas cards are full of novel ideas. He was the brother-in-law of Jenny Nyström and had received much of his training from her. She recommended him when she did not have time herself for all the commissions she received, but was not happy when she had to field complaints about his delays and carelessness. Georg Stoopendaal emigrated to the United States and even had a stint as a war correspondent in Cuba before he returned to Sweden. There were many artists in the Stoopendaal family including Jenny Nyström's husband, Daniel Stoopendaal, who sometimes helped her with her painting.

(AMALIA LINDEGREN). DANS I DALSTUGAN.

Hugs and Kisses

The Mistletoe The mistletoe has always had an aura of being somewhat magical. At Christmas it has been used, together with holly, as a form of protection on or above doors. In Sweden, where there is little holly, lingonberry twigs with strong leaves and red berries are the norm. The kissing under the mistletoe started in England and Swedes were quick to adopt the custom. But kisses could also be used as prizes in games. Hence, it is not surprising that they also made their way into Christmas cards.

Valentine Cards Quite a few of the kisses on cards have nothing whatsoever to do with Christmas. These cards are rather Valentine cards gone haywire. Celebrated on February 14, the St. Valentine celebration started in the Anglo-Saxon countries where anonymous expressions of love to somebody long admired from afar were sent on this day. The wishful thinking found expression in motifs of hugs and kisses. Swedish card producers added Christmas or Easter wishes to these motifs, as a St. Valentine celebration had not yet made it to Sweden. This gave rise to the Easter kiss and a whole new range of Christmas motifs.

Swedish Christmas Card Publishers It was Jenny Nyström who, while studying abroad, saw Christmas cards and alerted the venerable Bonnier publishing house about them. "They are very much in fashion abroad, and I think they would do well at home, where so much shabbiness of this kind is bought by the public," she argued. Bonniers was not interested, so Jenny

Previous page:

Jenny Nyström,
portrait of her son
Curt, Eskil Holm,
Stockholm 1911.

Jenny Nyström,
Eskil Holm,
Stokholm 1911.

Anonymous, C.N:s
Lj., Stockholm.

Anonymous, F.
1905–1910.

Nyström made her first designs for Eskil Holm in Stockholm and John Fröberg in Finspong. She had already painted a few originals for Wards in London, one of the largest card producers in Europe at the time. Eventually Axel Eliassons Konstförlag in Stockholm became the exclusive producer of Jenny Nyström cards and sells them to this day. Axel Eliasson had studied the very skilled German card producers before he, as a 22-year-old, set up his own publishing business. From a modest beginning in 1891, with a couple of motifs from Stockholm and Gothenburg, Axel Eliassons Konstförlag is today the only one of the many Swedish postcard producers with an unbroken tradition. Other pioneers were Tullbergs, Granbergs, and many others represented in this book.

The Widening of the Christmas Greeting

Holiday cards eventually developed into a real industry. In the 1950s, there was a reaction against the impersonal and formal habit of sending Christmas cards, but ironically this resulted in even more cards. Nineteen ninety-six was a top year for Christmas cards in Sweden with 62 million mailed. Since then there has been a steady drop with electronic greetings steadily gaining new ground. Many businesses have also replaced cards with diaries, calendars, or gift baskets. In the U.S., Christmas is still the biggest season for cards, with about 1.9 billion mailed each year.

H. Teschs, E.F.P.

Jenny Nyström,
without any
publisher's name,
1906.

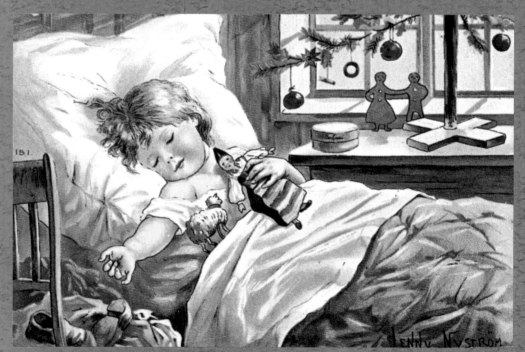

Magical Night   When the last of the sparklers
had died down and the last of the crackers
silenced, it was bedtime for the little ones. In the
olden days the family would sometimes bed down
in the straw on the floor on this magical night, to
leave the proper beds for the spirits of any dead
relatives. The husband was not allowed to sleep
next to his wife on this night. Candles were left to
burn for the spirits and perhaps plain and simply
because it felt good with some light on a dark night
such as this. What was left of the candles in the
morning was collected and used as medication
during the coming year. Candle wax was good
to have around to soothe a child's sore bum or
when the cow's teats needed smoothing. The
supernatural powers had complete control over
the magical Christmas night. Hence, it was best
to paint the sign of the cross on each door to stop
evil powers from entering the house. Before going
to bed, all tools had to be brought indoors because
otherwise they would be destroyed by the next
morning.

Predicting the Future   Ashes from the Christmas night fire, which were believed to have magical powers, were spread across the fields. It was not uncommon to rub some ashes on farm animals to prevent them from getting any diseases during the year. But before any ashes were collected, they had to be closely examined because they contained all kinds of valuable information about the coming year. If there were, for example, tracks in the ashes in the direction of the room, there would be an addition to the family. If the tracks were directed outward, there would be a death in the coming year. There were other ways to look into the future on Christmas night—at least for those who dared. The recommended way was the "year walk." It called for fasting on Christmas Eve (the very idea!) and then without uttering a single word, walking past seven churches and looking in through their keyholes. Everything that was observed on the walk home from the last church would have a significance for the coming year. That is, if it was interpreted correctly. The worst that could happen would be an encounter with the terrible, folkloristic *gloson* which was some kind of evil, Christmas pig. Its only function in life was to run in between the legs of a person and split him or her in two with its knife-sharp back.

Anonymous, PBF.

Jenny Nyström's: "John Blund", Axel Eliassons Konstförlag during the 19th century.

Aina Stenberg,
Eskil Holm,
Stockholm 1947.

Aina Stenberg,
Eski Holm,
Stockholm 1938.

Curt Nyström
Stoopendaal,
Axel Eliassons
Konstförlag,
Stockholm.

Aina Stenberg,
Eskil Holm,
Stockholm 1939
(73, 76).

Aina Stenberg,
Eskil Holm,
Stockholm 1934.

Aina Stenberg,
Eskil Holm,
Stockholm 1945.

Jenny Nyström,
Axel Eliassons
Konstförlag,
Stockholm.

Anonymous
1905–1910.

When Christmas Morning Glistens

The Early Morning Service   In the very early hours of Christmas morning, it was time for the trip to church. The horse was dressed up in its finest harness and was fastened to the splendidly decorated sled. Pitch torches were needed to show the way, because the church service, in certain places, started as early as 4 AM. Sleds with torches could be seen for miles around. Many towns and farms put lights on this morning. On arrival at church the torch was thrown into a large bonfire in the churchyard. It was important not to arrive too early, because the dead held their early morning service before the general one started. Indeed before sitting down the bench was wiped to take away any traces of earth left behind by the dead.

Jenny Nyström,
Axel Eliassons
Konstförlag,
Stockholm 1906.

Maja Synnergren
1941.

The Race   With the early morning service done with, it was time for a race. The belief was that the family that reached home first would also be the first to get the harvest in. To better the odds, farm hands were known to sneak out during the sermon and switch the harnesses of their competitors to cause a bit of confusion, and in that way, get a head start. Apart from this, the Christmas card motifs of the morning service project a feeling of peace. There are motifs where the Santas seemed to have made it to the church service. Jenny Nyström has painted one tomte helping to put up the hymn numbers inside, but her six Santas sitting outside the church, with a cauldron of *glögg*, look reassuringly heathen.

Adéle Söderberg,
Axel Eliassons
Konstförlag,
Stockholm 1912.

Jenny Nyström,
Axel Eliassons
Konstförlag,
Stockholm 1908.

Unsigned Jenny
Nyström card,
printed in Germany
in 1912.

Anonymous, A.V.,
Copenhagen 1903.

Photography,
R&K, 1913.

Jenny Nyström,
Axel Eliassons
Konstförlag,
Stockholm (of a
card first published
in 1899).

Opposite page:

C. Hall,
Eskil Holm,
Stockholm 1903.

Aina Stenberg,
Eskil Holm,
Stockholm 1947.

Jenny Nyström,
import without
name of producer.

Jenny Nyström,
Axel Eliassons
Konstförlag,
Stockholm 1912.

Anonymous, Joh.
Ol. Andreens
Konstförlag,
Göteborg 1905.

Anonymous.

Alna Stenberg,
Eskil Holm,
Stockholm 1950
(reprinted 1947,
1969, 1976).

Jenny Nyström,
John Fröberg,
Finspong.

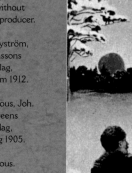

Be Greeted Both Master and Mistress

A Day of Rest Christmas Day was a day to rest at home after the hectic Christmas Eve and the early morning church service. No work was allowed on this day. Instead, Dad relaxed with Christmas magazines, like *Jultomten*, that all had a Santa taking the pride of place in their mastheads, while the children were busy with their gifts and the *Tomtepåsen* magazine full of games. The mother was in all likelihood busy in the kitchen, as usual, but hopefully she took a few breaks and indulged in the magazines *Christmas Mood* and *Mother's Christmas Letter*. No visits were allowed on Christmas Day, but the home was likely to be full anyway with extended family visiting. Anyone and everyone who could, spent the holiday with family and this included distant relatives as well as close friends.

Staffan's Ride On Boxing Day, it was once again time to get up early. The animals had not been taken care of on Christmas Day so there was lots to do. As their first task, farmhands rode out to exercise the horses that had been stabled for a long time. The horses were watered down in a north-flowing stream or spring for the sake of the magical power. Then the "Staffan's ride" would continue to the neighboring farms with the hope of getting a shot of aquavit and something good to eat. "Staffan Was a Stable Boy" was sung with a couple of improvised verses indicating what food and drink would hit the spot. If there was no hospitality forthcoming, the gang of riders would sometimes ride right into the house and help themselves.

En glad Jul

GOD JUL OCH GOTT NYTT ÅR!

Anonymous
(who has also drawn
Asian-looking
Santas) 1916.

Jenny Nyström,
Axel Eliassons
Konstförlag,
Stockholm 1915.

God Jul!

Jenny Nyström

Play House   It was not necessary to have a horse to ingratiate oneself with the neighboring farms. Maids and farmhands would also dress up and visit the farms, singing "Good Evening ye Master and Wife," for some eating and drinking. They would also collect food and drink for the communal dances to be held. Some dressed up as "star boys," but mostly the idea was to be unrecognizable. Sometimes the group would be accompanied by a Christmas goat in the form of one or more people hidden under a fur, maneuvering a ram's head with horns. Aquavit could be poured directly into the mouth of some of the more advanced goats, where the precious liquid was collected in a hidden bottle contraption.

Entertainment   In the olden days, people knew so many more games than we do today. There was never a dull moment. Charades, where one person acted out an old saying without uttering a word while the others tried to guess what it was, could go on for hours on end. There were so many games that were played with just fingers that to younger children looked like plain magic. Finger dexterity also developed into full shadow plays that were especially popular in the towns. Some performers were so talented that their acts developed into theatre productions. Cinemas did brisk business long before Donald Duck's Christmas Parade became a must for families with children in the 1950s.

M.I. Borg,
Axel Eliassons
Konstförlag,
Stockholm 1904.

Jenny Nyström,
Axel Eliassons
Konstförlag,
Stockholm 1973.

Anonymous 1907.

Jenny Nyström,
Axel Eliassons
Konstförlag,
Stockholm 1913.

Jenny Nyström,
Axel Eliassons
Konstförlag,
Stockholm 1909.

Jenny Nyström,
Axel Eliassons
Konstförlag,
Stockholm 1913.

Nyårshälsning från Ronneby

Happy New Year!

Symbols of Happiness The funniest New Year's cards are the ones with rose-colored dreams of the future. There is a veritable inflation in lucky symbols like galoshes, horseshoes, chimney sweepers, champagne, four-leaf clovers, and, above all, money. During the time of crisis, Jenny Nyström's little Santa even arrives with special lucky rationing cards, that guarantee happiness during the worst of circumstances. The biggest symbols of happiness, however, are the children that appear on so many of the cards. There are cards where Santa delivers both the newly born and the crib in the new year. On the other hand, bears on cards came with outstanding bills. But these two bears look so jovial that they could hardly be taking the debt all too seriously.

New Year's Cards Until 1915 in Sweden, New Year's cards were far more popular than Christmas cards. Today, the rare New Year's card is probably sent by someone in reciprocation for a Christmas card received. Generally, New Year's cards have been a bit more elegant and proper and sent to people with whom the relationship is more of a formal one. New Year's cards contained wishes and invocations for the future. Santa and the bliss he represented lived on in New Year's cards. This is not so strange as Santa, in his role as caretaker of the property, had a presence throughout the year. He was also the ruler of a Land of Happiness that is every person's dream.

Godt Nytt År. och en god fortsättning Tack för hortet. M. många hälsningar. Signe Assarsson

Godt nytt År tillönskar K. Svensson.

Godt Nytt Hel.

GOTT NYTT ÅR

Good Luck

Godt Nytt år!

Previous page:

Jenny Nyström, Axel Eliassons Konstförlag, Stockholm 1906.

Anonymous, Ernst Swensson, Ronneby before 1906.

The three cards on top were part of a longer series by K.V.i.B. from 1903–1906.

Anonymous.

Anonymous, likely British card.

E. Torsslow, Sv. Litograf AB.

Jenny Nyström,
Axel Eliassons
Konstförlag,
Stockholm 1907.

Anonymous, John
Fröberg, 1904.

Jenny Nyström,
Axel Eliassons
Konstförlag,
Stockholm 1910.

Jenny Nyström,
Axel Eliassons
Konstförlag,
Stockholm 1910.

Anonymous
German card from
WB & Co.

Aina Stenberg,
Eskil Holm,
Stockholm 1917.

Jenny Nyström,
Axel Eliassons
Konstförlag,
Stockholm.

Jenny Nyström,
Axel Eliassons
Konstförlag,
Stockholm 1909.

Jenny Nyström,
Axel Eliassons
Konstförlag,
Stockholm 1916.

Jenny Nyström,
Axel Eliassons
Konstförlag,
Stockholm.

Anonymous, EAS.

Anonymous.

Postscript

Sources   Most of the cards are from Anna-Lisa Cederlund's huge collection. The Aina Stenberg cards were lent by her daughter Karin Jansson MasOlle. Other cards are from Postmuseum, Nordiska Museet, and the author's own collection. The text has been updated by the author for this English translation. Apart from interviews and newspaper articles, the following books have served as sources:

Ehrensvärd, Ulla **Den Svenska Tomten** (Svenska Turistföreningens förlag 1979)

Ehrensvärd, Ulla **Gamla Vykort** (Bonniers 1972)

Holt, Tonie and Valmai **Picture Postcards of the Golden Age** (MacvGibbon & Kee, London 1971)

Jäder, Karl och Astrid **Jenny Nyström** (Gummesons 1975)

Keyland, Nils **Julbröd, Julbockar och Staffanssång** (Svenska Teknologföreningens förlag 1919)

Liedholm, Alf **Julens ABC** (Forum 1971)

Nilsson, Martin **Festdagar och Vardagar** (Norstedts & Söners Förlag 1925)

Olsson, Marianne (Editor) **Julen För 100 År Sedan** (Tre Tryckare 1964)

Swahn, Jan-Öjvind **God Jul!** (Bonniers 1966)

Tillhagen, Carl-Herman (Editor) **Glada Juledagar** (Tre Tryckare 1965)

White, Gleeson **Christmas Cards and Their Chief Designers** (London 1895)

Previous page:

Jenny Nyström, Axel
Eliassons Konstförlag,
Stockholm 1908.

Anonymous 1905–1910.

Next spread:

Aina Stenberg, Eskil Holm,
Stockholm 1939 (1967).

Jenny Nyström,
Axel Eliassons
Konstförlag, Stockholm 1916.

Jenny Nyström,
Axel Eliassons
Konstförlag, Stockholm 1913.

Collecting Christmas Cards

On December 23, 1939, an article in a Stockholm paper ended with the prophetic lines: "And we youngsters should perhaps consider collecting the Christmas cards of 1939. One day they will have a cultural value." The Christmas card is almost as old as the stamp and has now acquired a collector value. There are many devoted collectors in Sweden and abroad. Many Swedish cards fetch high prices at online and traditional auctions or at the specialized postcard antiquarians. Furthermore, Jenny Nyström's paintings as well as her Christmas card originals are highly coveted at auctions. This notwithstanding, the Christmas cards you received this year and the ones you may have kept are well worth a second look and perhaps even an album.

How to Date Cards

If it is hard to read the postmark on an older Swedish Christmas card, the back of the card can give you quite a bit of information. Until 1905, there was a designated space for name and address on the back of *Brefkortet* (see page 4). In 1900, the words *Carte Postale* were often added to *Brefkort*. After a spelling reform in 1906, most cards were spelled *Brevkort*. Between 1905 and 1910, *Brevkort* was sometimes translated into as many as 13 different languages. After 1910, there was just *Brevkort*, *Carte Postale*, or nothing at all. After 1930, there are sometimes series of numbers on the cards. The four numbers 3717, for example, tells you that the card was printed in 1937 and that the card was number 17 on the sheet. The number 225 on the other hand, shows a suggested retail price of SEK 2.25.